FRESHWATER
AQUARIUM
FISH

FRESHWATER
AQUARIUM
FISH

Grange
BOOKS

A QUANTUM BOOK

Published by Grange Books
an imprint of Grange Books Plc
The Grange
Kingsnorth Industrial Estate
Hoo, nr. Rochester
Kent ME3 9ND

1-84013-132-2

This book is produced by
Quantum Books Ltd
6 Blundell Street
London N7 9BH

Project Manager: Rebecca Kingsley
Project Editor: Judith Millidge
Design/Editorial: David Manson
Andy McColm, Maggie Manson

The material in this publication previously appeared in
The Tropical Marine Fish Survival Guide,
An Illustrated Encyclopedia of Aquarium Fish,
The Aquarium Fish Survival Manual

QUMSPFF
Set in Futura
Reproduced in Singapore by United Graphic Ltd
Printed in Singapore by Star Standard Industries (Pte) Ltd

Contents

UNDERSTANDING FRESHWATER FISH

Fish have managed to colonise most bodies of water, from the deepest oceans to the highest mountain pool. All you have to do is think about a place where you find water and it is virtually certain that you'll find a fish that lives in it.

Anatomy of Freshwater Fish

Water is much denser than air, so fish's bodies are streamlined to pass through it. Most fish have torpedo-shaped bodies to enable smoother swimming, but fish from fast waters have flat bodies and expanded fins to improve their stability in the rushing currents.

BASIC ANATOMY

A fish's body is usually covered by scales or thick skin which afford protection. Their fins keep them upright, and provide foward power and steering. In order to maintain a certain position in the water, a fish uses its gas-filled, swim bladder which extends from behind the head for about a third of the body length. Combined with fatty tissues it gives the fish lift. The great majority of fish breathe by extracting the dissolved oxygen from water passing over their gills. In these organs the blood vessels are close to the surface allowing oxygen to be absorbed and waste gases to be exchanged.

Left: The all-round vision of midwater fish helps to provide an early warning of danger.

Above: Corydoras sterbai uses its barbels to sift the sandy substrate for food.

TASTE AND SMELL

Although fish have nostrils, they are not used for breathing but for smelling. Fish can smell food from distance; but to taste it they have to touch it. There is no single organ of taste. Instead taste receptors are scattered across the head and body surface. Barbels are also covered in taste receptors which allow the fish to feel through the silty substrate until it touches food.

VISION

Most fish have eyes, although they don't have eyelids. The position of the eyes is an indicator of lifestyle. Bottom dwellers have eyes on the top of their heads while midwater fish have eyes on the sides of their heads to provide all-round vision. Some predators have developed binocular vision but the eyes of some cave-inhabiting species have regressed so that they are now blind.

Aquatic Environments

When we think of freshwater fish, we envisage the minnows in our local stream or the trout and salmon on the fishmonger's slab. However, anywhere there is water you will find fish adapting to their environment.

UNDERGROUND FISH

Much of our fresh water is stored in natural underground aquifers, yet in these seemingly inhospitable conditions we find fish which inhabit caves and live their whole lives in darkness. Even where these undergound water sources emerge as sulphurous hot springs there are fish to be found.

RAINY SEASON FISH

Many pools and small rivers are seasonal—they dry out each year and are only refilled by monsoon rains. These waters are generally slow-moving and low in oxygen, becoming progressively harder during evaporation. Killifish inhabit such seasonal pools and bury their fertilised eggs to survive the temporary drought.

Left: Even in the most inhospitable regions fish can be found.

Above: The Mudskipper needs a special brackish water aquarium with a shore-like beach area.

FOREST CREEK FISH

For the aquarist it is a challenge to try to re-create some of the environments in the home aquarium. A forest creek, for example, with leaf litter on the substrate, plants which grow out of the water and dappled lighting would be home to some of the Banjo Catfish, which mimic leaf litter, or to the Splash Tetras which lay eggs on the undersides of broad leaves above the water.

BRACKISH WATER FISH

Consider the brackish water regions where we find Mudskippers. An aquarium set up for these fish would utilise wood in the form of roots coming down into the water and a sloping silty wave-washed area for the fish to slither out onto where they can display to each other. In contrast, you may wish to keep the Archer Fish that will spit at insects from his watery lair.

Choosing an Aquarium

Just wandering round your local aquatic retailer will give you an idea of the number of different aquaria that are available. The question is, which one will enhance your home and provide the right environment for your fish?

SELECTING A TANK

The first thing to consider is size. The larger the aquarium, the easier it is to manage. However, the maximum size will be determined by the site you have available in your house. If possible, position the aquarium away from a heat source such as a radiator or where direct sunlight will fall on it. Alcoves are a popular choice but, with larger modern homes, aquaria are sometimes used as room dividers. If a ready-made tank is not quite the right shape or size, a custom-built aquarium may be ordered, although the cost is usually higher.

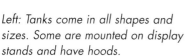

Left: Tanks come in all shapes and sizes. Some are mounted on display stands and have hoods.

Above: Rockwork in an aquarium can be dramatic— but very heavy. Make sure your tank is strong enough.

ACID AND ALKALI LEVELS

The degree of acidity or alkalinity of water is referred to as pH. The pH range is from 0 (very acid) to 14 (very alkaline), with 7 the mid-point being referred to as neutral. The pH scale is logarithmic, therefore a change of one unit represents a 10-fold change. Most fish need a pH range of 6.5–8.5. The individual pH level for each fish is given in the Fish Species section (see p. 16).

WATER HARDNESS

The degree of water hardness is graded by the amount of dissolved salts in the water and is referred to as °dH. The dH range is from 3° (very soft) to 25° (very hard). Most fish adapt to a range of 9–14°. However, some fish require very precise conditions, which must be provided, if you are to keep them successfully. Individual dH levels are given in the Fish Species section (see p. 16).

Decorating the Tank

What you use to decorate your aquarium is a purely personal choice. It will depend on the type of environment you wish to create. Dramatic effects can be achieved by using lots of different decorations, but be sure your tank is strong enough.

GRAVEL

Three sizes are available: fine grit, pea gravel and road surface gravel for larger aquaria.

ROCKS

Inert rocks such as slate, granite, and Westmoreland stone will not change the composition of your water.

Left: A well-planted tank needs only the addition of fish to bring it to life.

Above: For the best effects choose plants that complement each other.

WOOD

For versatility, wood is hard to beat in the aquarium. Not only is it decorative, it also provides an anchorage point for plants. For those who do not wish to use the real thing, realistic looking ceramic wood is available.

ARTIFICIAL PLANTS

Many of the artificial plants available today are so realistic that you can easily confuse them with the real thing. However, they are purely decorative and do not enhance the water quality of the aquarium or help combat any algal problems. Nevertheless,

they can look very attractive and provided your filtration system is well established there should be no problems.

LIVE PLANTS

In comparison, live plants can present more difficulties. First, you must carefully select truly aquatic species. Consider what you would do for garden plants. Plan your ideas on paper first and always leave sufficent space between individual plants for future growth. Make sure you plant them properly and give them sufficient light and good water conditions.

15

FISH
SPECIES

Key to symbols

The following icons are used throughout this directory to help provide a snapshot of the idiosyncrasies of each species.

Size. Maximum adult length in cm.

Herbivore. Should only be fed vegetable-based foods

Omnivore. Eats all types of aquarium foods

Predator. A meat-eater likely to attack other fish.

Single specimen. Should not be kept with others of the same species.

Community. Can be kept in groups of its own kind.

Safe with smaller fish. Even if large species itself.

ANABAS TESTUDINEUS

These fish can travel across land, on their pectoral fins, when their habitats dry up. They have been found up trees, which is where their common name comes from—Climbing Perch.

Family Anabantidae.
Common name Climbing Perch.
Distribution Malaysia, Indonesia, India, Southern China.
Size 22.5cm (9in).
Food Omnivorous. Flake, live, or frozen aquatic invertebrates, vegetable matter.
Temperature 22–28°C (72–82°F).
pH 7.0–8.0 **dH** to 25°.

BETTA IMBELLIS

Best kept in groups that include males and females. The males can be kept together but will engage in mock fights and displays, although little damage will be done to either fish.

Family Belontidae.
Common name None.
Distribution Indonesia.
Size 5cm (2in).
Food Omnivorous. Live food preferred but will take flake and frozen food.
Temperature 24–25°C (75–77°F).
pH 7.0 **dH** to 10°.

BELONTIA HASSELTI

A peaceful fish unless spawning, when males become pugnacious, and lose the lace-like pattern on the fins. The female should be removed after spawning takes place.

Family Belontidae.
Common name None.
Distribution Singapore, Sumatra, Java, Borneo.
Size 19cm (7.5in).
Food Omnivorous. Predominantly meaty foods, plus vegetable matter.
Temperature 25–28°C (77–82°F).
pH 6.5–8.0 **dH** to 35°.

BELONTIA SIGNATA

A very hardy fish, can be aggressive, and should only be placed with fish which can defend themselves. Males have an extended dorsal fin.

Family Belontidae.
Common name Combtail.
Distribution Sri Lanka.
Size 12.5cm (5in).
Food Omnivorous. Live food preferred flake, vegetable matter.
Temperature 24–28°C (75–82°F).
pH 6.5–7.5 **dH** to 25°.

COLISA LABIOSA

A good fish for the community aquarium. Should be kept as pairs. Males are more colourful and have a pointed dorsal fin.

Family Belontidae.
Common name Thick-lipped Gourami.
Distribution Northern India, Burma.
Size 9cm (3.5in).
Food Omnivorous. Live, flaked and frozen food plus vegetable matter.
Temperature 22–28°C (72–82°F).
pH 6.0–7.5 **dH** to 10°.

COLISA FASCIATA

A beautiful fish, for the community aquarium, which should be bought and kept as pairs. Males have elongated bodies, are more colourful and their dorsal fin ends in a point.

Family Belontidae.
Common name Banded Gourami, Indian Gourami.
Distribution India to Burma.
Size 10cm (4in).
Food Omnivorous. Live, flake, frozen food.
Temperature 22–28°C (72–82°F).
pH 6.0–7.5 **dH** to 15°.

MACROPODUS OCELLATUS

This fish is ideal for the home aquarium but is seldom imported. The male finnage is spectacular, both dorsal and anal fins are extended and the caudal is bright red-orange.

Family Belontidae.
Common name None.
Distribution Eastern China, Korea, Vietnam.
Size 7.5cm (3in).
Food Omnivorous. Live, flaked and frozen food.
Temperature 15–22°C (59–72°F).
pH 6.0–7.5 **dH** to 25°.

7.5

TRICHOGASTER LEERI

A wonderful fish for the larger community aquarium. Keep as pairs and they will display to each other, showing their true colours. Males show more red on the body.

Family Belontidae.
Common name Pearl, Gourami, Leeri.
Distribution Malaysia, Sumatra, Burma.
Size 11cm (4.5in)
Food Omnivorous. Flake, frozen, live and frozen food.
Temperature 24–28°C (75–82°F).
pH 6.5–8.0 **dH** to 30°.

11

PELTEOBAGRUS ORNATUS

P. ornatus is one of the few diurnally active Catfish. Its body is transparent to such a degree that not only are their internal organs visible, but so too are the body markings on the opposite side.

Family Bagridae.
Common name Dwarf Ornate Bagrid.
Distribution Malaysia and Indonesia.
Size 4cm (1.5in).
Food Insectivorous. Partial to *Daphnia* and *Tubifex*, will accept flake.
Temperature 22–25°C (72–77°F).
pH 6.5–7.2 **dH** 8–18°.

BROCHIS BRITSKII

This species has only been recently discovered, and is similarly coloured to the other two species of *Brochis*. Unique among the Callichthyidae, *B. britskii* has a bony shield that completely covers the underside of the head.

Family Callichthyidae.
Common name None.
Distribution Brazil.
Size 7.5cm (3in).
Food Omnivorous.
Temperature 22–25°C (72–77°F).
pH 6.7–7.2 **dH** 8–20°.

BROCHIS MULTIRADIATUS

The very distinctive snout helps differentiate this species from other Brochis species. Sexing is not known and there is no spawning record. This species is fond of digging in search of its food.

Family Callichthyidae.
Common name Hog-nosed Brochis.
Distribution Ecuador.
Size 9cm (3.5in).
Food Omnivorous.
Temperature 22–24°C (72–75°F).
pH 6.5–7.2 **dH** 8–20°.

BROCHIS SPLENDENS

This fish is often confused with *Corydoras aeneus*, the Bronze Corydoras, which is similarly pigmented. However, the longer dorsal fin of *Brochis*, and its larger size, distinguish the two.

Family Callichthyidae.
Common name Sailfin Corydoras.
Distribution Brazil, Peru, Ecuador.
Size 7.5cm (3in).
Food Omnivorous. Like small aquatic invertebrates, flake food.
Temperature 21–27°C (70–80°F).
pH 6.0–7.5 **dH** 6–25°.

CORYDORAS PANDA

Juvenile specimens are more markedly coloured than adults. *C. panda* is not so robust in captivity as other *Corydoras* species, requiring particular attention to water quality.

Family Callichthyidae.
Common name Panda Corydoras.
Distribution Peru.
Size 4cm (1.5in).
Food Omnivorous.
Temperature 22–26°C (72–79°F).
pH 6.5–7.5 **dH** 6–20°.

CORYDORAS BARBATUS

This is the largest species of the *Corydoras*. Those from the Rio de Janeiro area are more colourful, particularly the males which exhibit bright gold-yellow reticulations on the head.

Family Callichthyidae.
Common name Barbatus Catfish.
Distribution Brazil.
Size 6cm (2.5in).
Food Omnivorous.
Temperature 22–26°C (72–79°F)
pH 6.2–7.8 **dH** 4–25°.

DIANEMA LONGIBARBIS

Dianema are fairly peaceful, and not as boisterous as their *Hoplosternum* and *Callichthys* relatives. They are best kept in small groups of six or more, and tend to mope if isolated from others.

Family Callichthyidae.
Common name Porthole Catfish.
Distribution Peru.
Size 15cm (6in).
Food Omnivorous/Insectivorous.
Temperature 22–26°C (72–79°F).
pH 6.5–7.2 **dH** 7–20°.

DIANEMA UROSTRIATA

Clearly identifiable from *D. longibarbis* by the distinctive striped caudal fin. *D. urostriata* can also grow slightly larger than it. Both species are able to take in atmospheric air to supplement their oxygen supply.

Family Callichthyidae.
Common name Flag-tailed Catfish.
Distribution Brazil.
Size 15cm (6in).
Food Omnivorous/Insectivorous.
Temperature 22–26°C (72–79°F).
pH 6.2–7.2 **dH** 7–20°.

HOPLOSTERNUM LITTORALE

This is the largest member of the Callichthyidae family of Catfish. The slightly forked caudal fin helps distinguish this from other species of *Hoplosternum*.

Family Callichthyidae.
Common name None.
Distribution Northern South America.
Size 20cm (8in.)
Food Omnivorous.
Temperature 21–27°C (70–80°F).
pH 6.2–7.5 **dH** 8–20°.

HOPLOSTERNUM THORACATUM

Found in muddy stretches of rivers and streams, *H. thoracatum's* auxiliary intestinal breathing allows it to survive in poorly oxygenated water. Colouration varies considerably with this fish, dependent on its locality.

Family Callichthyidae.
Common name None.
Distribution Northern South America.
Size 17.5cm (7in).
Food Omnivorous.
Temperature 21–27°C (70–80°F).
pH 6.5–7.5 **dH** 6–22°.

AGAMYXIS PECTINIFRONS

A sedentary catfish that fits in well in a community aquarium of medium to large peaceful fish. It spends much of its time hiding away in caves or crevices in wood. Most active at dusk and in the night.

Family Doradidae.
Common name Spotted Doras.
Distribution Ecuador.
Size 14cm (5.5in).
Food Omnivorous. Flake, tablet, frozen, live food.
Temperature 21–26°C (70–79°F).
pH 5.5–7.5 **dH** to 12°.

AMBLYDORAS HANCOCKI

A fairly placid fish, *A. hancocki* can be kept in a community tank of similar sized fish. The common name alludes to the noises it produces when communicating.

Family Doradidae.
Common name Talking Catfish.
Distribution Northern South America.
Size 11cm (4.5in).
Food Omnivorous. Flake, commercial fish food.
Temperature 22–27°C (72–80°F).
pH 6.5–7.5 **dH** 8–16°.

MEGALODORUS IRWINI

Growth in the aquarium can be slow, but the fish is long-lived. As it grows, so too do the lateral plates and the thorn on each. The dorsal and pectoral fins are equipped with serrations.

Family Doradidae.
Common name Snail-eating Doradid.
Distribution Brazilian Amazon.
Size 60cm (24in).
Food Carnivorous. Snails, pelleted food, chopped earthworms, beef-heart.
Temperature 22–26°C (72–79°F).
pH 6.5–7.4 **dH** 7–20°.

HYPANCISTRUS ZEBRA

When photographs were first published of this fish, there was a rush by Catfish enthusiasts to obtain specimens. They have now become more readily available.

Family Loricariidae.
Common name Zebra Plec, L46.
Distributio Brazil.
Size 7.5cm (3in).
Food Omnivorous. Prefers meaty foods.
Temperature 22–27°C (72–80°F).
pH 6.4–7.0 **dH** 5–12°.

PANAQUE NIGROLINEATUS

Adult males can fight, using their interopercular spines as weapons. There are a number of variations of patterning which may be regional differences of the same species or new species in their own right.

Family Loricariidae.
Common name Pin-striped Plec.
Distribution Colombia.
Size 25cm (10in).
Food Herbivorous.
Temperature 22–26°C (72–79°F).
pH 6.5–7.5 **dH** 5–18°.

PIMELODUS PICTUS

The sharp pectoral and dorsal spines make it difficult to handle this fish. A net should never be used to catch these fish as the spines will become entangled and removal is difficult. Plastic bags are preferable.

Family Pimelodidae.
Common name Angelicus Pim.
Distribution Colombia.
Size 11cm (4.5in).
Food Insectivorous. Flake, tablet food.
Temperature 22–25°C (72–77°F).
pH 6.0–6.8 **dH** to 12°.

APHYOCHARAX ANISITSI

An undemanding shoal fish that may be kept in an unheated aquarium. However, if kept at the cooler end of its range the colours fade. A long-lived species and a good fish for the beginner.

Family Characidae.
Common name Bloodfin.
Distribution Argentina.
Size 5cm (2in).
Food Omnivorous. Small live or frozen food, flake.
Temperature 18–28°C (64–81°F).
pH 6.0–8.0 **dH** to 28°.

ASTYANAX FASCIATUS MEXICANUS

This fish is widely available in the hobby, far more so than its sighted counterpart. It is undemanding, should be kept in shoals and makes an excellent community fish.

Family Characidae.
Common name Blind Cavefish.
Distribution Texas, Mexico, Panama.
Size 9cm (3.5in).
Food Omnivorous. Flake, live or frozen food.
Temperature 22–25°C (72–77°F).
pH 6.0–8.0 **dH** to 30°.

CHALCEUS MACROLEPIDOTUS

A large predatory Characin for the specialist. Easy to keep in a large tank, but fit a tight cover because the fish are prone to jumping. Can be kept with fish of a similar size.

Family Characidae.
Common name Pink-tailed Chalceus.
Distribution Northern South America.
Size 25cm (10in).
Food Carnivorous. Takes meat, fish and tablet food.
Temperature 23–27°C (73–81°F).
pH 6.5–7.5 **dH** to 18°.

CORYNOPOMA RIISEI

A gentle shoaling fish for the community aquarium. Can be difficult to acclimatise, but once used to aquarium conditions it is very robust. Males have longer pectoral fins.

Family Characidae.
Common name Swordtail Characin.
Distribution Colombia.
Size 6cm (2.5in).
Food Omnivorous. Live, flake and frozen food.
Temperature 22–27°C (72–81°F).
pH 6.0–7.5 **dH** to 25°.

GYMNOCORYMBUS SOCOLOFI

Juveniles, up to 4cm (1.5in) long, are very attractive and active; their unpaired fins are red-orange in colour. However, this fades with maturity and the fish become more sedate.

Family Characidae.
Common name Socolof's Tetra.
Distribution Colombia.
Size 5cm (2in).
Food Omnivorous. Flake, insect larvae, vegetable matter.
Temperature 22–26°C (72–79°F).
pH 5.5–7.5 **dH** to 20°.

HEMMIGRAMMUS ERYTHROZONUS

Peaceful, shoaling fish for the planted community aquarium. Males are slimmer than females. This fish is bred commercially in large numbers. It is friendly with its own species and safe with smaller fish.

Family Characidae.
Common name Glowlight Tetra.
Distribution Guyana.
Size 4cm (1.5in).
Food Omnivorous. Flake, insect larvae.
Temperature 22–26°C (72–79°F).
pH 6.0–7.5 **dH** to 15°.

CHARACINS

HEMIGRAMMUS ULREYI

A timid fish when first introduced into the aquarium. Needs plenty of space and the company of other peaceful species. They display their best colours when seen in sunlight.

Family Characidae.
Common name Ulrey's Tetra.
Distribution Paraguay.
Size 5cm (2in).
Food Omnivorous. Flake, insect larvae, and small aquatic invertebrates.
Temperature 23–27°C (73–81°F).
pH 6.0–7.0 **dH** to 10°.

HYPHESSOBRYCON PULCHRIPINNIS

A pretty shoaling fish for the community aquarium, always swimming about. It is friendly with its own species and safe with smaller fish as well. Males have a black edge to the anal fin.

Family Characidae.
Common name Lemon Tetra.
Distribution Peru.
Size 5cm (2in).
Food Omnivorous. Live, frozen, flake.
Temperature 23–27°C (73–81°F).
pH 6.0–7.5 **dH** to 20°.

MOENKHAUSIA PITTERI

A shoaling fish for the well-planted community aquarium. Feed well on live foods such as *Daphnia*, blood-worm, and mosquito larvae, or frozen substitutes.

Family Characidae.
Common name Diamond Tetra.
Distribution Venezuela.
Size 6cm (2.5in).
Food Omnivorous. Flake, live *Daphnia,* small frozen invertebrates.
Temperature 24–28°C (75–82°F).
pH 5.5–7.0 **dH** 4–10°.

PARACHEIRODON INNESI

Probably the most popular of all aquarium fish, Neons are bred in vast numbers and tolerate a wide range of aquarium conditions. Males are slim and have a straight blue line.

Family Characidae.
Common name Neon Tetra.
Distribution Peru.
Size 4cm (1.5in).
Food Omnivorous. Flake, insect larvae, small frozen invertebrates.
Temperature 20–26°C (68–79°F).
pH 7.0 **dH** to 20°.

CHARACIDIUM RACHOVII

Peaceful with other fish. Loach-like in its habits and movements. Males have a spotted dorsal fin; females have a transparent dorsal fin.

Family Characidae.
Common name None.
Distribution Southern Brazil.
Size 7.5cm (3in)
Food Carnivorous. Tablet food, live or frozen insect larvae.
Temperature 20–24°C (68–75°F).
pH 5.5–7.5 **dH** to 24°.

CURIMATA SPILURA

Very peaceful fish for the larger community aquarium, provided that the plants are hardy enough to withstand the onslaught. Copious amounts of green foods should be offered.

Family Curimatidae.
Common name Diamond-spot Curimata.
Distribution South America.
Size 9cm (3.5in).
Food Herbivorous. Vegetable foods, but will take flake.
Temperature 21–27°C (70–81°).
pH 6.0–7.5 **dH** to 25°.

CHARACINS

AEQUIDENS RIVULATUS

Noted for its aggression, they should be kept only with fish able to fend for themselves. They take up territories and will defend them especially when breeding. Males are generally larger, females are darker in colour.

Family Cichlidae.
Common name Green Terror.
Distribution Ecuador, Peru.
Size 20cm (8in).
Food Omnivorous. Live food if possible, will take flake or frozen food.
Temperature 21–24°C (70–75°F).
pH 6.5–7.5 **dH** to 15°.

AMPHILOPHUS ALFARI

Variations can be seen in the colour, body, and finnage shape of this fish, even in fish from the same river system. In the aquarium it is domineering and also likes to dig in the substrate. Males are much larger than females.

Family Cichlidae.
Common name Pastel Cichlid.
Distribution Central America.
Size 22.5cm (9in).
Food Omnivorous. Live, flake, frozen food.
Temperature 23–26°C (73–79°F).
pH 6.5–7.0 **dH** to 10°.

AMPHILOPHUS CITRINELLUS

This is a rather belligerent fish especially when breeding. They love to dig and move large quantities of gravel around the aquarium, so plants in the aquarium are a waste of space.

Family Cichlidae.
Common name Midas Cichlid.
Distribution Central America.
Size 30cm (12in).
Food Omnivorous. Live, flake, frozen.
Temperature 23–26°C (73–79°F).
pH 6.5–7.0 **dH** to 10°.

APISTOGRAMMA BORELLII

A beautiful fish that makes a lovely addition to a well-balanced, community aquarium of very peaceful fish. These creatures are territorial but problems only arise when they are breeding.

Family Cichlidae.
Common name Borelli's Dwarf Cichlid.
Distribution S. America.
Size 7.5cm (3in).
Food Carnivorous. Small live food.
Temperature 24–25°C (75–77°F).
pH 6.0–6.5 **dH** to 12°.

APISTOGRAMMA CACATUOIDES

This fish derives its names from the extended rays at the beginning of the dorsal fin. Males are much larger than females and have longer fins. Keep several females with each male.

Family Cichlidae.
Common name Cockatoo Dwarf Cichlid.
Distribution Brazil.
Size 9cm (3.5in).
Food Carnivorous. Live food, flake.
Temperature 24–25°C (75–77°F).
pH 7.0 **dH** to 10°.

APISTOGRAMMA MACMASTERI

A delightful fish that has a wonderful territorial defensive display which can be seen quite often if the group is kept with a few other peaceful fish. Males are larger, the caudal is bright red.

Family Cichlidae.
Common name Macmaster's Dwarf Cichlid.
Distribution Venezuela.
Size 7.5cm (3in).
Food Carnivorous. Live food.
Temperature 24–30°C (75–86°F).
pH 6.0–6.5 **dH** to 8°.

APISTOGRAMMA NIJSSENI

A very beautiful fish that only shows its true potential if the correct water conditions can be maintained. Males are larger and colourful. Peaceful and may be kept with other fish.

Family Cichlidae.
Common name Nijssen's Dwarf Cichlid, Panda Dwarf Cichlid.
Distribution Peru.
Size 6cm (2.5in).
Food Carnivorous. Live food, flake, frozen.
Temperature 24–30°C (75–86°F).
pH 5.5 **dH** below 5°.

APISTOGRAMMA STEINDACHNERI

Only aggressive when spawning, these fish may be housed with other fish, but be prepared for the other fish to be herded to one section of the aquarium if the Cichlids breed. Males are larger and more colourful.

Family Cichlidae.
Common name Steindachner's Dwarf Cichlid.
Distribution Guyana.
Size 10cm (4in).
Food Carnivorous. Live food.
Temperature 23–25°C (73–77°F).
pH 6.0–7.0 **dH** to 10°.

ARCHOCENTRUS NIGROFASCIATUS

An undemanding fish, but it is belligerent towards other fish and is therefore
most suited to a species aquarium. They
pair off and spawn readily. There is an
albino variety of this fish.

Family Cichlidae.
Common name Convict Cichlid,
Zebra Cichlid.
Distribution Central America.
Size 15cm (6in).
Food Omnivorous. Live, flake, frozen,
green food.
Temperature 20–24°C (68–75°F).
pH 6.5–8.0 **dH** to 20°.

ARCHOCENTRUS SPILURUS

Very peaceful, they will breed regularly
if conditions are right. Males are larger
with a pointed dorsal and ventral fins.
Mature males have a bump on their
foreheads.

Family Cichlidae.
Common name None.
Distribution Guatemala.
Size 11cm (4.5in).
Food Omnivorous. Live, flake, frozen,
green food.
Temperature 22–25°C (72–77°F).
pH 6.5–7.5 **dH** to 12°.

ASTATOTILAPIA BURTONI

A territorial and quarrelsome fish with its own kind that lives quietly with other species. Keep several females with each male.

Family Cichlidae.
Common name Burton's Mouthbreeder.
Distribution East and Central Africa.
Size 11cm (4.5in).
Food Omnivorous. Live, flake, frozen, green food.
Temperature 20–24°C (68–75°F).
pH 8.0–9.0 **dH** to 20°.

AULONOCARA BAENSCHI

The males of this striking fish are yellow and blue, the degree of one or other of the colours depends on the locality the fish are from. Peaceable and suitable for most community aquaria.

Family Cichlidae.
Common name Baensch's Peacock, Yellow Regal Cichild.
Distribution Malawi.
Size 10cm (4in).
Food Omnivorous. Live, flake, frozen food.
Temperature 22–25°C (72–77°F).
pH 7.5–8.5 **dH** to 25°.

CICHLIDS

41

CICHLIDS

CICHLASOMA PORTALEGRENSIS

A hardy fish well suited to beginners, they are easy to keep, feed, and breed. It is not easy to tell the sexes unless the fish are ready to breed, males tend to be greenish in colour while the female is brownish.

Family Cichlidae.
Common name Brown Acara, Port Acara.
Distribution Brazil, Bolivia, Paraguay.
Size 15cm (6in).
Food Omnivorous. Live, flake, frozen.
Temperature 19–24°C (66–75°F).
pH 6.0–7.0 **dH** to 10°.

CLEITHRACARA MARONII

Commercially bred, they are now becoming so inbred that their size has diminished. A peaceful fish, it is ideal for a larger community aquarium.

Family Cichlidae.
Common name Keyhole Cichlid.
Distribution Guyana.
Size 15cm (6in).
Food Omnivorous. Live, flake, frozen food.
Temperature 22–25°C (72–77°).
pH 6.0–8.0 **dH** to 20°.

COPORA NICARAGUENSIS

In the main peaceful, *C. nicaraguensis* is a very beautiful fish that can be kept with other species. Their one drawback is that they eat some plants.

Family Cichlidae.
Common name Nicaragua Cichild.
Distribution Nicaragua, Cost Rica.
Size 25cm (10in).
Food Omnivorous. Live, flake, frozen food.
Temperature 23–26°C (73–79°F).
pH 7.0–8.0 **dH** to 15°.

CYPRICHROMIS LEPTOSOMA

A shoaling fish, it requires a lot of swimming space in the upper levels of the aquarium. It may be kept with other Cichilds as it is quite peaceful. Males are brownish with yellow tips to the pectoral fins.

Family Cichlidae.
Common name None.
Distribution Tanzania.
Size 14cm (5.5in).
Food Omnivorous. Live, flake, frozen food.
Temperature 23–25°C (73–77°F).
pH 8.0–9.0 **dH** to 20°.

C
I
C
H
L
I
D
S

GEOPHAGUS BRASILIENSIS

Although territorial, it is fairly tolerant of other fish. These fish are best left to pair themselves since, if the pair is incompatible, they may keep eating the eggs.

Family Cichlidae.
Common name Pearl Cichild.
Distribution Eastern Brazil.
Size 27.5cm (11in).
Food Omnivorous. Live, flake, frozen food.
Temperature 20–23°C (68–73°F).
pH 6.5–7.0 **dH** to 10°.

HEROTILAPIA MULTISPINOSA

These fish are like chameleons, they change colour according to their mood. It is difficult to tell the sexes even though the male's fins tend to be pointed and longer.

Family Cichlidae.
Common name None.
Distribution Panama, Nicaragua.
Size 12.5cm (5in).
Food Omnivorous. Live, flake, frozen, green food.
Temperature 22–25°C (72–77°F).
pH 7.0 **dH** to 10°.

PSEUDOTROPHEUS SOCOLOFI

This peaceful creature is only defensive when breeding. The easiest way to tell the sexes is by the egg spots on the anal fin of the male.

Family Cichlidae.
Common name Eduard's Mbuna.
Distribution Malawi.
Size 11cm (4.5in).
Food Omnivorous. Live, flake, frozen food.
Temperature 24–26°C (75–79°F).
pH 8.0–8.5 **dH** to 18°.

SATANOPERCA ACUTICEPS

A beautiful, non-aggressive Cichild whose only drawback is that it likes to dig, it my be kept with other peaceful fish. Males have extended dorsal and anal fins.

Family Cichlidae.
Common name Sparkling Geophagus.
Distribution Brazil.
Size 25cm (10in).
Food Omnivorous. Live, flake, frozen, green food.
Temperature 24–26°C (75–79°F).
pH 6.5–7.0 **dH** to 12°.

HOMALOPTERA ORTHOGONIATA

Very peaceful with other fish; with each other there may be mock fights but no damage is done. They spend much time grazing through algae and over flat rocks and leaves.

Family Balitoridae.
Common name Saddled Hillstream Loach.
Distribution Indonesia, Thailand.
Size 11cm (4.5in).
Food Omnivorous. Aufwuchs, bloodworms.
Temperature 20–24°C (68–75°F).
pH 7.0 **dH** to 10°.

BOTIA BERDMOREI

A boisterous fish, it can be aggressive to its own kind and others, preventing them from feeding. When irate it may make clicking noises. Take care when handling.

Family Cobitidae.
Common name None.
Distribution Burma, Thailand.
Size 15cm (6in).
Food Omnivorous. Flake, frozen, live food.
Temperature 22–26°C (72–79°F).
pH 6.5–7.5 **dH** to 15°.

BOTIA MACRACANTHUS

A social Loach that should be kept in groups. It is active by day, and a worthy occupant for any community aquarium. The species is prone to White Spot.

Family Cobitidae.
Common name Clown Loach.
Distribution India, Sumatra, Borneo.
Size 15cm (6in).
Food Omnivorous. Flake, frozen, tablet, live foods.
Temperature 25–30°C (77–86°F).
pH 6.0–6.5 **dH** to 12°.

BARBUS BIMACULATUS

Classic shoaling fish that likes the company of its own kind. Kept in groups they will swim out in the open, but kept as solitary specimens or pairs they tend to retire to the darker recesses.

Family Cyprinidae.
Common name Two-Spot Barb.
Distribution Sri Lanka.
Size 7.5cm (3in).
Food Omnivorous. Flake, frozen, live food.
Temperature 22–24°C (72–75°F).
pH 6.5–7.0 **dH** to 15°.

BARBUS LINEATUS

A very active shoaling fish that should be kept in groups of 10 or more. The lines on the male's body are more pronounced and he is slimmer than the female.

Family Cyprinidae.
Common name Striped Barb.
Distribution Malayasia.
Size 11cm (4.5in).
Food Omnivorous. Flake, frozen, live and green food.
Temperature 21–24°C (70–75°F).
pH 6.0–6.5 **dH** to 10°.

BARBUS SCHWANEFELDI

Although sold in great numbers for community aquaria, they are not really suited to this. They grow large and are very active. They are ideal when kept as a shoal in very large display tanks.

Family Cyprinidae.
Common name Tinfoil Barb, Schwanefeld's Barb.
Distribution S.E. Asia.
Size 35cm (14in).
Food Omnivorous. Flake, frozen, live and green food.
Temperature 22–25°C (72–77°F).
pH 6.5–7.0 **dH** to 10°.

BARBUS RHOMBOOCELLATUS

Seldom imported, this fish seems to do well in soft, slightly acidic water. When healthy and fed lots of live foods, these fish have an almost iridescent sheen on their body.

Family Cyprinidae.
Common name None.
Distribution Borneo.
Size 5cm (2in).
Food Omnivorous. Live foods or flake.
Temperature 23–28°C (73–82°F).
pH 6.5–7.5 **dH** to 10°.

BARBUS TICTO

Ideally suited to a community aquarium, these fish are undemanding. They can take cooler conditions in the winter but before doing this check that your other fish can tolerate such low conditions.

Family Cyprinidae.
Common name Ticto Barb, Two-Spot Barb.
Distribution India, Sri Lanka.
Size 10cm (4in).
Food Omnivorous. Flake, frozen, live foods.
Temperature 19–22°C (66–72°F).
pH 6.5 **dH** to 10°.

BRACHYDANIO NIGROFASCIATUS

These seem to prefer warmer waters than other *Brachydanio* species. Keep them as a shoal. Males are slimmer and their anal fin has a dark brown edge, which can appear golden.

Family Cyprinidae.
Common name Spotted Danio.
Distribution Burma.
Size 5cm (2in).
Food Omnivorous. Flake, frozen, live food.
Temperature 24–28°C (75–82°F).
pH 6.5–7.0 **dH** to 12°.

5

CYCLOCHEILICHTHYS JANTHOCHIR

An active fish, it likes plenty of space to swim in. Generally peaceful toward fish of a similar size. It makes an excellent companion for peaceful, bottom dwelling Catfish.

Family Cyprinidae.
Common name None.
Distribution Indonesia, Borneo.
Size 20cm (8in).
Food Omnivorous. Flake, frozen, live food.
Temperature 22–26°C (72–79°F).
pH 6.0–6.5 **dH** to 8°.

20

DANIO AEQUIPINNATUS

An excellent fish for the larger community aquarium. Keep in shoals of males and females. Males are slimmer, more intensely coloured and have a blue stripe.

Family Cyprinidae.
Common name Giant Danio.
Distribution India, Sri Lanka.
Size 10cm (4in).
Food Omnivorous. Flake, frozen, live and vegetable food.
Temperature 22–24°C (72–75°F).
pH 6.0–7.0 **dH** to 12°.

NOTROPIS LUTRENSIS

A cold water fish, it is becoming more and more popular for the aquarium. Keep as a shoal. In the wild they live in moderately flowing streams which have a gravel or sand substrate.

Family Cyprinidae.
Common name Shiner.
Distribution Midwest USA.
Size 9cm (3.5in).
Food Omnivorous. Flake, frozen, live food.
Temperature 15–24°C (59–75°F).
pH 7.0–7.5 **dH** to 18°.

OPSARISIUM CHRYSTYI

A very attractive fish but seldom imported, it should be kept in groups. A
surface dweller, it will jump at the least
provocation. The colours in sunlight are
unbelievable.

Family Cyprinidae.
Common name None.
Distribution Northern Ghana.
Size 15cm (6in).
Food Carnivorous. Aquatic inverte-
brates, insects or flake.
Temperature 22–24°C (72–75°F).
pH 6.5 **dH** to 10°.

PARLUCIOSOMA CEPHALOTAENIA

Classic shoaling fish that is often over-
looked for the large community
aquarium. It should be kept in groups
of six or more individuals. Males are
slimmer than females.

Family Cyprinidae.
Common name Porthole Rasbora.
Distribution S.E.Asia.
Size 14cm (5.5in).
Food Omnivorous. Flake, frozen, live
food.
Temperature 22–24°C (72–75°F).
pH 6.0–6.5 **dH** to 15°.

RASBORA EINTHOVENII

A shoaling fish for the community aquarium. It is only possible to tell males and females apart during the breeding season. At this time males are smaller and slimmer.

Family Cyprinidae.
Common name Long-Band Rasbora.
Distribution S.E.Asia.
Size 7.5cm (3in).
Food Omnivorous. Live, flake and frozen food.
Temperature 22–25°C (72–77°F).
pH 6.0–6.5 **dH** to 8°.

RASBORA RETICULATA

A very attractive fish for the large community aquarium with open water and compatible with other peaceable fish of a similar size. Good glass cover is needed as they may jump.

Family Cyprinidae.
Common name Net Rasbora.
Distribution Sumatra.
Size 6cm (2.5in).
Food Omnivorous. Flake, frozen, live food.
Temperature 22–26°C (72–79°F).
pH 6.0–6.5 **dH** to 10°.

APHYOSEMION AUSTRALE

One of the most frequently seen killies, and an excellent fish for the softwater community aquarium. Males are far more colourful than females, and have extended finnage.

Family Aplocheilidae.
Common name Cape Lopez Lyretail.
Distribution West Africa.
Size 6cm (2.5in).
Food Omnivorous. Prefer live food but will take flake.
Temperature 21–24°C (70–75°F).
pH 5.5–6.5 **dH** to 10°.

APHYOSEMION CALLIURUM

Males can be quarrelsome with other males of their own kind. Females are plain in comparison with the highly coloured males.

Family Aplocheilidae.
Common name Red-Seam Killie.
Distribution West Africa.
Size 5cm (2in).
Food Carnivorous. Will take flake and frozen food.
Temperature 24–26°C (75–79°F).
pH 6.5–7.0 **dH** to 15°.

APHYOSEMION SCHMITTI

These are peaceful fish that may be kept with others of a similar nature. Males are exceedingly colourful, whereas females are brown with faint red spots.

Family Aplocheilidae.
Common name Schmitt's Killie.
Distribution Liberia.
Size 6cm (2.5in).
Food Carnivorous. All small live food.
Temperature 22–24°C (72–75°F).
pH 6.0–6.5 **dH** to 8°.

APHYOSEMION GERYI

Easy to keep, this attractive fish may be placed in a community aquarium. Males are more colourful than females. However, different populations have differing degrees of colouration.

Family Aplocheilidae.
Common name None.
Distribution West Africa.
Size 5cm (2in).
Food Carnivorous. Prefer live food but will take flake and frozen.
Temperature 22–26°C (72–79°F).
pH 5.5–6.5 **dH** to 10°.

BRACHYRHAPHIS EPISCOPI

A beautiful little livebearer, but very difficult to maintain for any length of time in captivity. It is susceptible to disease, so aquarium hygiene is all important.

Family Poecilidae.
Common name Bishop Brachy.
Distribution Central America.
Size 4cm (1.5in).
Food Carnivorous. All small live food, sometimes frozen food.
Temperature 24–26°C (75–79°F).
pH 7.0–8.0 **dH** 4–20°.

GAMBUSIA AFFINIS

Gregarious and undemanding, it may may be kept with other similar fish. Its almost insatiable appetite for mosquito larvae has lead this fish to be widely used for malaria control.

Family Poecilidae.
Common name Western Mosquitofish.
Distribution Texas.
Size 4cm (1.5in).
Food Carnivorous. Prefer live mosquito larvae but will take flake and frozen.
Temperature 18–24°C (64–75°F).
pH 6.0–8.0 **dH** to 30°.

GIRARDINUS FALCATUS

Very tolerant of most water conditions, this fish may be kept with other peaceful fish. Its name refers to the sickle-shaped gonopodium of the males.

Family Poecilidae.
Common name Yellow Belly.
Distribution Western Cuba.
Size 5cm (2in).
Food Omnivorous. Flake, frozen, live and green food.
Temperature 24–29°C (75–84°F).
pH 6.0–8.0 **dH** to 25°.

LIMIA VITTATA

An excellent fish for the hard water community aquarium. Males are more colourful, with black and gold spangles. Females have less intense colouration.

Family Poecilidae.
Common name Cuban Limia.
Distribution Cuba.
Size 11cm (4.5in).
Food Omnivorous. Algae, aquatic invertebrates, flake.
Temperature 22–26°C (72–79°F).
pH 7.5–8.5 **dH** 8–30°.

POECILIA LATIPINNA

A species which has been cultivated to produce various colour forms. Suitable for a hard-water community aquarium, but best kept in brackish or marine water.

Family Poecilidae.
Common name Sailfin Molly.
Distribution Southern USA.
Size 10cm (4in).
Food Omnivorous. Algae, plant material plus live food and flake.
Temperature 20–28°C (68–82°F).
pH 7.5–8.5 **dH** 10–30°.

 10

POECILIA RETICULATA

A highly adaptable fish that is a firm favourite among novices. Bred by the millions in fish farms, Guppies have been hybridised to give larger finnage on males.

Family Poecilidae.
Common name Guppy, Millionsfish.
Distribution Central America, Brazil.
Size 6cm (2.5in).
Food Omnivorous. Small aquatic invertebrates, flake.
Temperature 18–27°C (64–81°F).
pH 7.0–8.5 **dH** 4–30°.

 6

XIPHOPHORUS MACULATUS

The ideal community fish, peaceful and fecund. Its young will even grow to maturity in a community tank. Many variant colour forms have been produced.

Family Poecilidae.
Common name Southern Platy.
Distribution E. coast of Mexico, Guatemala, Honduras.
Size 10cm (4in).
Food Omnivorous. Small aquatic invertebrates, flake.
Temperature 22–26°C (72–79°F).
pH 7.0–8.0 **dH** 8–35°.

10

XIPHOPHORUS VARIATUS

A classic community fish. It can even be kept at low temperatures in an unheated aquarium, provided it is acclimatised to these conditions slowly.

Family Poecilidae.
Common name Variable Platy.
Distribution Southern Mexico.
Size 5cm (2in).
Food Omnivorous. Small aquatic invertebrates, flake.
Temperature 15–25°C (59–77°F).
pH 7.0–8.0 **dH** 8–35°.

5

CHILATHERINA AXELRODI

An active fish which displays well when kept as a shoal of males and females. Males are more colourful than females. Keep in a community aquarium with plenty of open water.

Family Melanotaeniidae.
Common name Axelrod's Rainbow.
Distribution Papua New Guinea.
Size 9cm (3.5in).
Food Omnivorous. Takes flake, frozen and live food.
Temperature 25–28°C (77–82°F).
pH 7.0–8.0 **dH** 12°.

CHILATHERINA FASCIATA

A rather attractive Rainbow, it likes brightly lit conditions, being found in areas of streams where sunlight falls. Males are larger and more colourful than females.

Family Melanotaeniidae.
Common name Barred Rainbow.
Distribution Northern New Guinea.
Size 11cm (4.5in).
Food Omnivorous. Prefers live food.
Temperature 27–30°C (81–86°F).
pH 7.0–8.0 **dH** to 10°.

GLOSSOLEPIS MACULOSUS

One of the smaller Rainbowfish, they may be combined with other peaceful fish. Keep them in shoals and pay careful attention to water quality. The spots appear at two to three months old.

Family Melanotaeniidae.
Common name Spotted Rainbow.
Distribution Papua New Guinea.
Size 5cm (2in).
Food Omnivorous. Takes flake, frozen and algae.
Temperature 24–26°C (75–79°F).
pH 7.5 **dH** to 12°.

MELANOTAENIA HERBERTAXELRODI

A peaceful shoaling fish. Males are deeper in the body and more colourful than females. The best colours are shown in sunlight.

Family Melanotaeniidae.
Common name Lake Tebera Rainbow.
Distribution Papua New Guinea.
Size 9cm (3.5in).
Food Omnivorous. Takes flake, frozen and live food.
Temperature 21–25°C (70–77°F).
pH 7.5–8.0 **dH** 10–15°.

MELANOTAENIA LACUSTRIS

Very eyecatching, these fish make a wonderful focal point in an aquarium. Males have the more intense blue colouration. Unfortunately this colour fades slightly with successive captive-bred generations.

Family Melanotaeniidae.
Common name Lake Kutubu Rainbow.
Distribution Papua New Guinea.
Size 10cm (4in).
Food Omnivorous. Takes flake, frozen and live food.
Temperature 24–26°C (75–79°F).
pH 7.0–7.5 **dH** about 12°.

MELANOTAENIA PARKINSONI

Keep these active fish in a shoal. These are one of the easier Rainbows to keep, and they breed readily in the community aquarium.

Family Melanotaeniidae.
Common name Parkinson's Rainbow.
Distribution Papua New Guinea.
Size 11cm (4.5in).
Food Omnivorous. Prefers live food but takes flake and frozen.
Temperature 26–29°C (79–84°F).
pH 7.5–8.0 **dH** 8–15°.

Index

Alphabetical listing of scientific names.

Index of common names

I N D E X